MASKS

For Annette, Joe and Lucas.

MASKS

Duncan Bush

SEREN

SEREN
is the book imprint of
Poetry Wales Press Ltd.
Andmar House, Tondu Road
Bridgend, Mid Glamorgan

© Duncan Bush, 1994

ISBN: 1-85411-105-1

*The publisher acknowledges the financial assistance of the
Welsh Arts Council.*

Cover: Painting `Three Studies of an Egyptian Bust'
by David Gould, watercolour, 27x14.5", 1986.

Back cover photograph of Duncan Bush by David Ahmed.

Contents

European Capital

The Dream Poem of the South African Mercenary

1. Hotel Léopold

I wake in some old White Star liner in the heart
of Brussels. Glimmers of panelled teak
in windowlight along a maze
of tilted corridors to find a bathroom.

Lettered porcelain. Brass taps. Then
the hotel barber brings moist hot cloths
to soften my stubble. He bears a metal
tray like a dentist's (comb, scissors,

circumcision knife). He unwraps my face
and tilts my chin back, shears me
like an Easter lamb. A lift opens. I drop
a doorkey at a desk. It's night

again. The city opens. I'm in the red-light streets.
The girls wait in lit windows, bored
as bald dress-shop mannequins. One sits knitting
even. But I am not excited by such

homeliness. I have a wife at home
who knits. I go for
the black in leopardskin lycra.
Without the speckled dress, shoes, wig

she is the more leopard: small round-cropped
skull, shoulders muscled for speed.
After what these good Belgians did
to her country and its people,

can it matter what you or I do with her?
Her pink palate arches
open like a cat's yawn. Her supple
teak glimmers in the indirect lighting.

2. Rue du Congrès

Lit streets desolate as motorways. A bar, blue
curaçao; then coffee acrid as chewed feverfew.
I long for cold neon, the chattering machines
and silent players of amusement emporia

where the rent boys wear *lederhosen*
and even the women have one shoulder
developed from playing, playing, every pull
exercise-training, rehearsal

for the sudden, torrential big kill.
My lagging heel — the right — prints
a neat, blocked *D* of blood
along the pavement, but the trail

freezes before I gain the boulevards.
At night the Stadhuis
is a vulgar, half-lit wedding-cake.
Two tiny figures — the man a *maître d'hôtel*

and his bride a Christmas angel —
rotate and glide like skaters
to a tinny, endless automatic
music somewhere in its heart.

It's bitterest mid-December. In the lit window
of some vast department store
a stiff waxwork Nativity has drawn
fewer spectators than the Birth.

Loudspeakers churn out *Silent Night*
in scratchy *flamand*. Two kings are bearded.
Jews, the other Nubian black. They bring
guns, uncut heroin and myrrh.

3. Café Europa

These Brussels burghers swim like slow fish
in their long café aquariums. My dream, too,
is long, silt-heavy as the Congo.
A man dressed like a groom ignites

the *crêpes-suzette*, then turns them
deftly in the swift, meths-purple flame.
The happy couple watch him, pressing
palms together in soundless

smiled applause of expectation. I limp
past to another bar-sign glowing red
as a cigar-end at a junction.
Inside, two men play billiards

on a royal-blue cloth. The tables over here
lack pockets, and I've no small change in mine
— only a sheaf of ornate bonds in copper.
One man looks up, chalking, as I gain the counter,

and they speak across the balls in Dutch
or Afrikaans. I was in Amsterdam once, too —
streetnames all *J*'s and *K*'s, words
ugly, consonantal as a code. I had a Flemish girl

called Simkje there. She wasn't in the book.
Her long red hair dragged
like a bloodied mop across
the bathroom lino, to and fro: the black and

white squares of a draughts-board or
a Vermeer interior, *Le Billet Doux*,
which I had paused before that very
morning in the Rijksmuseum.

4. Rue de la Loi

I order blonde beer from the blonde, choose
a cheroot and rasp a match
with a red head. The English brogue I gently place
on the worn footrail throbs, and makes

a moist, vulvo-vaginal sound. It has filled
slowly with my blood. But is it a crime
to have your own blood
on you? Besides, the knife is in the river,

and the river's in the sea. One day
perhaps my milk-blue Swede masseuse
will coyly ask me to explain
the pale scar on my thigh. I too will

smile mysteriously, and tell her I was
in Katanga with the Paras when the trouble
flared. How we took Hammarskjöld out of the air
at 20,000 feet. I change soles on the brass

rail, turning to watch these louts chasing
a red ball with two whites to fluke,
in time, a cannon. Grey smoke I exhale
towards the table drifts and clouds

under the shade — my dark-sopped trouser-cuff,
the brimming shoe, are in its light, like Harry Lime's.
A table stares, then two, then all. I am
the thicket and the fleece-caught ram.

Beneath the suburbs, I know, lie the sewers
and the rats; above, the stars'
immense fixed wheel... (Vienna too, though,
was another city, in another time.)

La Vie Des Grandes Courtisanes

Even Jeanne Duval's a subject for theses
— a product which rhymes uniquely with *faeces*.
(*La Mulâtresse stupide, infidèle et avide...*
Yet *divine et bestiale* — a mix one can adore —
according to de Banville, Théodore.)

No one can explain this halfbreed cocotte's life
by raw Parisian fogs and lost *cocotiers*,
not even the pitiable, later famous man who loved her
for a month, an instant or a year —
each having no choice but to be
at once the bleeding wound, the bloodied knife.

Farmer's Widow, Tawe Valley

One

Down steep oakwoods old as the coal,
under the floating buzzard's mew
I still walk with the collie
and his speckled hazel stick. I can't

not love this shaggy river-valley
below the three poor, hummocky fields
we farmed, now just the few
sheep in them, or crows.

Gone the club moss and swamp palm
and the fern my father
found, perfect in the anthracite,
the mile or two downriver

where he lost his lungs.
Gone a tropical primordium, like
the frontier boom-days of those pits.
Gone to bulldozed blue shale

uplands of Forestry replanting,
some Alaska of perennial
shade-all, soil-souring
river-embittering conifer,

and a few last, leased private mines,
walking horses in and out
of the drift still, some of them:
a cave, a small black downward dune

of waste high on the valley's side:
the old deciduous woods decayed,
decayed and fallen buried
there, so much prehistory.

Two

Sometimes, after the mudded paths
fade, I walk and walk
on through these woods
like someone swimming out

to sea.... Today, unsunned marshy
bottom-land I cross through
freezes as I tread it
in a 3 o'clock December dusk,

mire re-stiffening to a crackle
underfoot. Then the dog trots on
while I halt, staring to wonder
at some indefatigable zeal there is

in mindless harm. You'd think
they — kids, I know,
from the post-war council rows
of miners' families or unemployed

along the valley floor, kids
probably no older than
the tree, boys running rough
and purposeless with puberty —

must have half-hacked, half-gnawed
the birch down with a tyre lever
or some old coal-house axe
as dull. Then, its own weight

felling it, bored finally,
had let it lie, persisting
not enough even to trim and
shoulder it back home to saw

to lengths for burning.
And the pointlessness of it all
brings tears into my eyes.
Such things despair me now.

Three

The new year runs down to a raw
east wind all February,
a leaking barn:
chapped hands, chapped lips.

And, living off a lightbulb's heat,
these yellow-smirched few
wobbly, frost-born lambs,
the ewes eating the afterbirth.

While I stand watching them and
thinking, Nature eats up
everything. But only people have to
feed off their own hearts.

Four

A cold April day I come again
upon the sapling, lying
now in still-tender thorns
of bramble, the new Spring grass.

Its twigs are dry, unbudding
as a besom. Though the unicorn-silver
stiff-arced, hewn stump brims a
tacky milk: I smell it, taste

it from my fingers. And
that tearful, quick pang wells
up again now through me
for the tree and for this

season's sap still
coming, coming. As this knobbed
stick strains to leaf
in my tight hand.

For The Hawk Fallen

The hobby was moustached,
rakish, brilliant
of eye.

The most aerial of the falcons,
it reduces
to a shuttlecock

of pinions
wind-aflutter
at the kerbside

of a country road.
And what bears it off is this
long colony of ants.

Brigitte Bardot In Grangetown

Off Ferry Road, the toilet of a garage where
the mechanics come at lunch to cut the hands' grease
with green Swarfega jelly, glancing once

at themselves in the rust-foxed mirror, and then
go in to eat brought sandwiches and play
pontoon with the soft, soiled pack,

three walls of the cubicle sporting the odd grey
newsprint pin-up, some *Kay* or *Tracy*,
alike as playing cards,

and then a whole closed door facing you (if
ever you sat over the stained bowl)
or Bardot as she was at twenty,

and thirty-five, and is now, in her smiling
puppy-fat fifties, still corn-blonde,
and then more of her

again (with one of Ian Rush) out where they eat,
over the workbench's oil and
hacksaw-dust, the clenched vice.

The boy who put all hers up was a six-month
Government trainee. A bit simple, they all thought.
A headbanger, the fat one said.

He had a thing about her, the boy, grinning
foolishly, half-proudly, when they kidded him, told him
she was old enough to be

his mother. *That slag?* the fat one said once.
*Look at her. She's anybody's. Even saving baby seals
all she knows how to do*

is lie down with one. And laughed: soft, smirched face
looking at that photo, then at the one of her
naked, hands raised as if to pin or

loose her hair, the honey-hued still-teenage
body, milky Mediterranean behind her, evening.
He left the other week,

the trainee. He didn't finish, he never even came
back for his tools. So now they're
anybody's like the photos:

like, the fat one knows, the photos always are.

A.I.D.S. (The Movie)

Those now-cultish horror movies
from the 'Fifties always were

two-edged to the discerning buff.
In small-town married America

when the alien seed-pods fell
to breed, mutate, occupy human form,

invading *Body Snatchers* spelled
Reds even Inside The Beds, to some;

to others, zombefied neighbours
wandering muzak-eerie shopping malls —

collectivised twin nightmares
where a *Living Dead* walked

almost indistinguishable from
us and their former selves....

Now, past consumerist parable
and Cold War paranoia,

the anxious heart must yearn
back to more hopeful filmic models —

like the old bio-pics re-shown
wet Sunday afternoons in winter,

monochrome *Lives* of the Great
Scientists (Paul Muni as Pasteur,

Montgomery Clift as Freud) — images
of the lone obsessive,

still-uncelebrated
hope of all the ailing world,

stooped at the altar of the cure's
discovery: that private, half-lit

melodrama of a desk lamp nightly
on past dawn.... Oscar nomination,

like the Nobel Prize, are down
as certainties. (But Fleming has

first to have discovered penicillin,
and Mme. Curie — prior to Greer Garson —

radium: the miraculous, hard-won
salvific, glowing in the dark.)

Late Night Hotel Room
With Japanese Transistor Radio

While the satellite dishes spread the sign of
the benighted household
and the pound in your pocket
sinks and twitches like a quaint barometer,

this wanly cosy world seems barely to have changed
since families crouched to the Home Service:
burred walnut-veneer
art deco casings curved like Gaumonts

with their dim-lit window of exotic wavelengths
(Kalundborg, Algiers and Hilversum)
and dust-fluffed
valves behind the set....

Now, turning from tonight's flaunting inanities
of team-show hosts and unseen
talking heads addressing the nation's bungalows
you slide

the fluorescent-green band sideways through
a surging gabbled blur of
faint and foreign speech —
Oslo palm-court quartets, French Elvis Presleys

(straight off the Van Allen Belt, stations unknown
by daylight) — to settle
in a dated, bleak nostalgia:
Radio 2's insomniac dance-bands

still playing
middle-of-the-road late night muzak
for a million glow-lit
dashboards and a dozen rented rooms...

the green band
twitters swiftly back to 4 in time for
the once-famous voice to read the last instalment of
The Book At Bedtime....

This is the terrible
dark night of the mind, where it's not even 11:30
and there's no TV:
the atavistic hour, the Ovaltine

hour, closer to death than sleep, than
whisky-coma....
Desperate, you sit
and listen with Disgusted, Tunbridge Wells.

There is a single naked 60-watt electric lightbulb burning
somewhere in your head.

Writing By Streetlight

St. John of the Cross speaks of
that awful dark night in
the soul when it's
always three in the morning....

It's 3 a.m. at King's Cross
too, for homeless men with
bundles, a boy
with a torn Tesco bag,

the old mad woman
effing and blinding, screaming
at the two young police
that she had better men

than them sons lost in war,
et cetera. Outside's
the street: streetlights
snow-humped cars, pavements

like the surface of the moon.
The capital quivers
like the farmost star
in stellar cold, waste

electricity. It's 3:05.
And this February day
dawn's not
till 8:19. Waiting for it

in a doorway, all that's
clutching you to life's
your own wrapped
arms. And the dark

night of the soul's as nothing:
sounding brass and tinkling
symbol. On the street
the ice-wind is enough

to bring tears to your eyes.
And the long night of the body
is what kills,
what terrifies.

Old Master

This minor Dutch master always
existed for the Xmas card — the expensive
kind (for the expensive

friends), on good gloss board,
under at Art House imprint. His depiction
of these wintry woods

is remarkable for detail, verisimilitude
and light. How cold it looks, with that
sombre, greenish sky, and

not the tiniest distal twig on those
bare oaks unfurred with snow
over the frozen pond

to which a stag has come. Yet curiously
what this prospect strikes
into the heart is

warmth, like the first whisky's.
For (propped now with robin redbreasts
vintage cars and

santaclauses over glowing hearths —
just as it once hung, single,
in some Haarlem

burgher's drawing-room) the rawness of
that wan and waning daylight
only sharpens,

as through a window, looking out,
vicarious and comfortable confirmation
of the Great Indoors...

even, a ghost-breath'd and admiring poor
nosing the pane like cattle
at a milking-gate.

(For these the picture's meaning lies,
though, in its inmost enigma.
They are present, imaged

by the stag come to a woodside pool
to drink, only to find it paved,
hard with that sheet of

glaucous, marvellously-rendered ice.)

Crocuses

In the seconds after
the knock he may have
tried to burn the poem
that would kill him. But
words are hard to
kill. Print turned
silvery as the page went black.

They put him in the big
house on the outskirts with
white bedsteads and no
windows. But word
went down the heating pipes,
leaked out through
even screamproofed walls.

In the end someone probably
shot him on a train
going east, or just off it,
and hid the body in the
ground. Here and there his
words came slowly up like
crocuses, in winter.

Living In Real Times

Summer, 1993

In Queen St., Cardiff, I halt to watch in a choice
of screens an over of the Trent Bridge test,
Shane Warne looping wristspin in at
some tailender doomed at best to time-serving

till stumps. Between padded-off balls the eye flickers
to the other channel banked in
other sets, headlines unspooling soundless
beyond Curry's window, the newsreader's mouthings:

a street elsewhere foreshortened
by the long lens. Someone running in the tottering
apologetic way the very frightened run,
as if to panic and sprint could only serve

unfailingly to draw the sniper's bullet. Now
someone whom that bullet has already found. He lies
sprawled amid the usual crazed, cradling women
like one adored at last beyond all dreams.

Sarajevo? Mostar? Vukovar?...TV's intimate and
generalising eye makes everywhere somewhere else:
a province of that small, remote country
of which we, famously, know little

still. While post-modernism makes all things
present, all things post-reality (from the intensity
of this particular and very private grief I realise
I saw these shots two hours ago). Again

the street, down which no doubt the dead man too
had run. Past those same bins, the burned-out
truck, between the building's cover and
a water standpipe. Running partway

then throwing his hands up at it all
and falling dead just at that piece of broken kerb....
As he falls over and over again now in the women's
keening, or in some syndicated twenty-second

filmclip replayed over the next day's news.
Night-time, street, streetlight, a chemist's shop,
wrote Alexander Blok as Russia came apart
(that is, the first time round):

whatever you come to, wherever
you go, it all comes down at last
to this. *You'll die, and just as always start
the dance again.* Over and over. And forever

and for ever. No *Amen.* While from the other end,
on another set, Merv Hughes — that moustache
bigger than Nietzsche's — takes the wicket,
a jubilant slip hurling high the catch, fieldsmen

throwing up their hands, the hangdog batsman
turning away, reluctant as a stood-up groom:
live now, sudden, in real time.
And I wait automatically, lingering

to watch them all do it again, in slowmo,
almost missing it the first time,
trained to the instant replay and the freezeframe:
to the destined fact, knowing there's no way out.

The Sunday The Power Went Off

In a darkening house we sat,
room-light gone, television shrunk
mid-shout to a speck then

nothing, even the old fridge's
whir and periodic
judder stilled,

and saw each other in
flashlit instants while
my five-year-old elder son

counted the sulphur-violet
dimness and I with him:
One. Two. Three. Four. Five:

a second for each year
of his life, and the sum for every
mile as slowly the storm

moved off to a horizon
of rumbles from that sudden
crack in the sky that seemed

right over the roof-ridge
like a rifle-shot amplifying
down a badlands canyon

in movies, the one-off, perfect shot
bringing a man unexpectedly down
forever, though the sunlight

unimpaired, the reel
unfinished, the shocked wildlife
listening a second more then

resuming its tiny business
of survival, even the dead man's
riderless skewbald reaching down to

browse the seeding grass.
Storms now scare me almost more than
my half-scared, half-excited kids,

if only for that first, premonitory
skyquake, distant and dull
as a range of hills or

that dark low cloud like hills
you get at dusk; or for that
faint first flash I know

may any time come before a roar
as of wind and of whirlwind,
finding me sitting

in this same stone house or bending
in the sunlit garden, knowing
instantly under clear air

this wasn't lightning, seeing
wife, sons, sunlight suddenly
reversed, as in a negative,

and simply waiting with them there,
too scared this time to count.

Just A Few Things Daddy Knows About Ice

for Lucas

Starts from water. Starts at zero. Flashes
flow to brittleness. Tightens
as the mercury drops, then cracks
glass. Aspires to the Absolute
Cold of Minus 273
(asymptotic constant like light's speed.
pi's final decimal):
point at which the world
shivers to bits.

More banally:
kills off the dinosaur.
Sinks the unsinkable.
Turns the waterfall to stone
and the moisture of your own outbreath
in the air to a tinkle
of falling motes the Russian language
calls the music of the stars.
And clinks in whisky.

Keeps its secret for millenia,
holding the second flood
in the dam, the white continent. Holding
us under the Pole
while weather warms
and the mapped coasts are on the rocks.

After Chernobyl

Long February of snow and redwing
blown faint with
cold out of the east.

Fields halfway into April still
the colourlessness
of chewed-out cud.

Now in May late sycamore leaves
— maroon-delicate —
unfolding out of the bud

while at night I listen to a flicker
at the window of
Spring rain and radiation,

thinking of the Esquimaux
lasting each
glacier-slow Arctic winter

on the essential, the
survivor's, faith:
We do not believe. We fear.

Seventy Thousand Hillbillies

Arkansas

Even the professors down here
drive pickups to class,
have names like Mary Sue or Billy Bob.
Clinton voters, they're no rednecks.

Maybe it's protective
local colouring, hedged in by
the Survivalists out in the bush
with their razor-wire,

booby traps and bunkered arsenals:
plugged into Revelations
like country music on a Walkman, they're
less into the *lex talionis*

than the pre-emptive strike.
I see a rear-window sticker *Nuke
The Whales*, then a personalised
registration plate *INSANE.*

In Craighead County, one
professor tells me, Billy Hill's
a common name. Look in the directory,
he says, there are

thirty, forty. They're all
listed as *Hill, Billy.*
He leans to scratch his shin
above the Wolverine boot, times

it, grins, and says The truth is there
are hell of a lot more than that.

On The Appalachian Trail

Eastern Kentucky

"Bloody" Harlan's fondest birthright
is still the Right To Bear
Arms; and use them.
Out on some grit road, from

a crawling Dodge, these Good Old Boys
'll meet your eye and slowly raise a hand,
a loaded blue Colt
in the dash....

But most places you go in Appalachia
Heritage looks what
it is all over:
denizen tourism.

In the roadside Art Outlets
taped homeboy bluegrass vies
with handmade
kitsch: once parochialism

gets shown
its own face
in the mirror it's no
use for anything

except a passing trade.
This isn't hinterland Wales; these
pits aren't yet Labour Museums.
But with a Company union,

the *Longwall* one-man computer-
operated shearer down
the mine, and mechanised "Mountaintip
Removal" above ground,

craftwork and local colourists
look like the one sure
future here too. Even
the saw-toothed knuckledusters

in the Harlan County Gun Store
count as handcraft
(though that's to get around the law).
Brass Paperweights,

they come at a snug
6 oz. and retail at $8.50.

Postcards From Zakinthos

1. The Safe Couples

Hung-over, each swim at morning's
a rebirth. You can push a pedalo. Or
just lie, watch one repeatedly topple

from a sailboard in shallows — tyro
windsurfer obsessive as a comic drunk;
as his pink, cancerous tan.

The lunchtime *ouzo* clouds milky
with water from a cold-fogged carafe.
Heat or honeymoon ignite the afternoon

to sexsweats and siesta in a room.

2. The Small Turtles

At Laganas Bay tiny loggerhead turtles,
backs still moist-soft, crawl first towards
light, the great mother: glitter

off sea. But hatching out at night they
turn inland, struggling up the sloped
beach of dry sand. Step through them

at morning, some curious atavistic
invasion — all dead
on dehydration, still headed for

the bright pulse of the new disco bars.

The News Of Patroclus

His silence hissed like gas
in the tent, in silences
between the messenger's apprehensive,
useless, lamentatory words.

He gestured, and the man was gone
at last; the tent-flap
dropped. He sat.
He had forgotten

everything: the shouts, the burning
ships, old Agamemnon's
virgin concubine;
his own hand-picked harem

of handmaidens on a rota,
and the daydream
of the sea-trip home.... Henceforward,
when a girl fell slack and dying

for the glory of his touch
he knew only a corpse.
Like those hurt in love, he had been
hurt so much

he had become invulnerable.
He sat. Then flung
away the lyre and armed
and slung the short sword at his thigh.

He went out to the hard, pure light,
the dust, the oaktree
and the Skaian gate,
stooping quickly to retighten

the loosened sandal at his heel of clay.

Coming Back

Le vieux Paris n'est plus (la forme d'une ville
Change plus vite, hélas! que le coeur d'un mortel).
                              Baudelaire

One

Every time you come back
it's shrunk again, as if
the railings had closed in
on the park, or

the roads had shortened
their perspectives;
as if the hills had come
nearer like clouds.

It's not only what had not
been there, nor what's
missing: once all of this
seemed vast, was known.

Suddenly farness of things,
the space they occupy, is
altered here,
is unimaginably less

than memory. And everything
is bigger than this suburb
you were born in, even
the one you have to live in now.

Two

The slow shock of almost
full crowns where there'd once
been splinted saplings
is no more than that of

one old, suddenly remembered
tree leaning in the park's hedge
which is still that
set of easy hand-holds

and bark steps your own repeated
climbing helped wear
to this ribbed gloss. And you
see that tree — long suffering

and safe, like an old horse —
is still tree, and boyhood
boyhood, while you've
changed more than the city.

Three

The blue grammar-school
Oxford atlas fitted,
like any other book, into
your new tan satchel then.

Oceans were hyacinth,
and mountain ranges rose fawn
through ochre-browns to violet
to the ice-cap white of

permanent high snow —
shadow-crannied, printed
so they looked
embossed on the page.

It was here you
dreamed America, immense Siberia,
the night-dark
Sundam Trench;

flew over lion-coloured
desert, bluffed
like builder's sand
dry-trickling down its own

escarpments; or traced
blue, mudless
rivers to some greenly
fertile coastal strip —

landscapes pictorial
and actual, not
symbolic. And now you have
come back here, and,

unmanned, suddenly awash
in the unmapped particular, find you
know every kerb and gatepost,
that shaggy hedge of

dusty privet or suburban
laurel, the little striped
snails in the crumbling walling,
a manufacturer's name still

stamped on the old cast-iron
cover of a drain.
And your own sons'
childhood doesn't

stop your heart more or
more suddenly than coming
back, forty, to this road you
once walked down to school.

Are There Still Wolves In Pennsylvania?

*A poem sequence in ten parts
for two voices*

A dramatised adaptation of this sequence
was first broadcast on BBC Radio 3 on
October 23rd, 1990.

Wesley: William Hope
Linda: Shelley Thompson
Produced by: Alison Hindell

1.

(Wesley Reece Ball)

Scar

I've got it still, this star-shaped
scar on my left shoulder
which I won't
outlive. Which I

forget about, unless
I'm soaping in the shower
or, sometimes,
with my wife. My

little star-shaped scar,
my scar-shaped star.
My purple Star.
My planeride home.

Our own frag-blast, which burned,
then ached, like hell. And then
itched worse. I finger you
under my shirt.

I know you like my own prick.
Little wrinkled seam,
you're my good luck:
out of all that flying air,

a chance wound big and
deep enough to save,
within this beer-loosened
bag, at least my life.

2.

(Linda Ellen Ball)

Veteran's Wife

The times he fills his
head with this
shit. Odd nights, but
even now, 1988,

weekends especially.
Stuff, okay, we one time
both of us
liked: The Doors,

say: *The End.* But that one
track over and over
again, drinking, staring,
like he sees his

own death, and all those
American boys', and
those slants', through Jim
Morrison, his. Or like

on the winter break
to Paris, Père Lachaise
in the snow,
and we looked for Jim's

grave, brushing it
off flat stones to read
them till
our gloves sopped, and I

looked too, because, well,
let's face
it he was beautiful, once
there wasn't a girl

who wouldn't have
in West Virginia (all
this of course was previous
to this A.I.D.S.. Long previous),

though they do say
he got fat in the end. And Wes
said when we didn't find
it down the ninety-third

damn alley we must have
gone down between the dead,
"It's not as if
I have a flower to

lay on him anyway
out of it all."
Not like, though he never
said it, he laid a flower,

one rose, at that black wall
in Washington, all *those* names.
But we found that one.
And he put his hands on

the marble, crying between
his arms, as if he
could have shoved it back,
like he wanted

to let them all out or
go in there with him, with Lee,
who I never met and sure as
hell never now will.

And I loved him again then,
though I didn't know.
But I can't
handle it sometimes still

now twenty years on, twenty
years. It's not the whores.
I forgave him
the whores and bargirls

long ago, Saigon, Hue city,
Singapore. I forgive
him the dead. I wasn't there.
It's just what I can't

forgive him is, I've had to
live with him and
all he knows is he should
have died out there too.

3.
(Wesley Reece Ball)

Hunting Trip

If we had a boy
maybe I would take
him too. But now it's just
me, the once or

twice in a year I
have to do it, be
out here in a one-man pup
tent overnight,

the loaded gun next to
my head, hardly
sleeping, still scared
of being alone

in the dark at
almost forty,
the wild dark and noises of
woods still so huge

you'd never crash a way
out, no matter what
the panic.
So just a waiting

for the long grey
cold of dawn
when you can find
a way back,

no compass, just following
a thread of water downhill
to some stream or river,
settlement.

Somehow I seem to need to be
scared, to find
my own way
clear on that thread. Out here

all that's going to kill me,
I know, is
other men, or
maybe a cottonmouth.

But it's as if I need
to give myself that
chance, have
them find me

two days or two weeks
too late, black with ants,
sprawled, face
eaten away.... I think often

of those guys
up in Washington State, who
live in the forests all year
alone, in compounds.

Who came out of 'Nam, the jungle
just long enough to know
they never could
live again in a town or

even a house, something
in them wasn't fit,
and being scareder
of themselves,

I guess, than of any
other man or snake or
prowling bear
alive, or any

woods at night,
knowing
the wild, the dark
was in them, theirs.

4.
(Linda Ellen Ball)

Aphrodisiac

And so I wonder what
the hell he knows,
and how much.
Because I thought something

when I saw him
going through my purse,
and I knew it
wasn't the goddam car keys

he was looking for, like
he said, but, I don't
know, maybe
my diaphragm

or a rubber or,
who knows, something
real corny like a
booklet of matches

from Best Western
Motel.... But I
knew it for
sure before he went

hunting this morning, and
he came up behind
me and held me again, swaying,
and we ended up doing it

for the fourth time
these two days,
hot as when we met —
or hotter, because

we're better at it
now, or ought to be,
good Christ, all them
thousands and thousands of

times we must have
done it down the years....
And I said after, as
we were lying there:

*What in hell's turning
you on so much lately?*
And he got up and
put his arms into his shirt

and, as he was buttoning
it, looked
back at me and shrugged and
just said: *Jealousy.*

5.
(Wesley Reece Ball)

Memories of Graduation, 1972

Night's so big around,
light from these stone-ringed
embers almost spooks me.
Are there still wolves

in the Commonwealth
of Pennsylvania?
— or just those evil yellow
slant eyes

in the Disney movie:
shining, circling, always
hungry out there at
the edge of total dark?

Like Sgt. Ripley used to say,
Some motherfucker
always watching,
and it ain't de Lord.

That other black kid
— what was his name?
:Coop —
from Gulfport Mississip.,

he lit a Chesterfield
one night on watch,
took one pull, and
before the smoke

could come double out of it,
Victor Charlie shot the tip clean
off his nose,
two hundred yards away.

An easier shot, I fry the thawed
steak from my backpack,
tip beans in
with it, eat it

from the pan. Food
tastes like nothing
in the open air
like this, washed down

with bourbon. I've eaten
too damn often squatted
on my heels on trails.
Memory's some net

the little things get caught in
and the big slip through.
Half-drunk, I recall the afternoon
I graduated out of Pitt,

and I wandered off
still eating from a frat
barbecue to talk to that
young Physics major

on the grass. I had
the scroll to frame,
those letters to my name —
the first

in my whole family or kin
since Adam. I asked
her way too soon,
What's your name? — though

I knew it. And she smiled
too soon, too secret,
so I knew she'd
soon as not not tell me.

She held her books
tight against her chest.
I still had a plate, the empty
plastic glass.

Louise, she said. We
swing our feet
one at a time, so slow,
towards the library. I knew

it: she was already going
going gone, like all
the women went — water
from a too tense-clenched hand.

She was polite enough to
ask, *What's yours?* And I
was weird and lost enough
to tell her: *G.I. Bill.*

6.

(Linda Ellen Ball)

After The Hunting

I watch Wes look to
clean his buck-knife somewhere
from the doe.
There's no rag

save them old, pale Levis
he keeps on
wearing and me washing
though one knee's

a web of strings. *Who*
wears jeans with
holes in any more? I tell him.
This ain't the 60s.

Though to look at him,
that hair, that Custer beard,
you'd swear it still was.
When he come Home

his hair was short as the fur
on that deer's muzzle.
It lies there
where he heaved it

off the pickup's tailgate.
Its legs are straight,
the little hooves
together. He squats instead

and runs the blade in
and out in the dirt.
Nothing'll clean a knife
like good earth, he says.

He's full of sayings.
Like that time he
drew his finger though
the hare's blood,

sucked it clean. *That's what*
the Indians do,
he said. *Or used to. Take on*
the spirit of the thing

you killed. The speed.
i.e.: Me Big Hunter. Huh.
Men are such kids. But
later I thought,

yeah, but how do you get
rid of them spirits afterwards?
When they're men's,
or kids'? Can the Indians

tell you that? Or
the Joiner Center in Boston?
Because they're in him
still, like that tick is

in our elmtree.
You can't see it. But
that tree's dying,
leaf by leaf.

And I can't
care any more. They're his,
not mine. And tonight
he's at the mill.

Tonight he's at the mill.
Each night
this week I'm almost sorry
when he goes. Because.

Because because because.
But I can't hardly
wait for him to leave.
And I do

wish now that I'd
bought them salmon
cord pants
in Gibson's Discount

in the end. Even if they was
as tight as spandex.
You got a mean little butt, honey,
Jack told me in the trailer.

Like two goose eggs
in a handkerchief. Come here.
I love it
when he does it

that way. From the pickup cab
Midnight Train To Georgia
surges, fades,
through static from

them power lines. Wes straightens
like his knee-joints are gone
stiff. He folds the blade.
The cats can have

this mess, he says. It's
wet and pink and brown. *Why
don't you fucking bury it,* I say,
and go inside. Kids,

that's all: the money
they work to squander
on a craze: a rifle,
or a cartridge belt or

a collector's knife:
all for a meat he don't even
truly favour. All to
shoot and gut and skin

that thing out in the yard,
a small grey
whitetail
deer, not even carrying horns.

7.
(Wesley Reece Ball)

Night Shifts

At midnight I tell the foreman
I ain't well and frank
my card. And
it's true. I ain't. I know

this crouching here in the treeline,
binoculars
round my neck. Anything,
though, 's better

than going through the washing
basket coming
off the shift at dawn.
The shotgun's on the back seat.

When I loaded the shells
I thought of
him putting it in.
One time. And then

again.... And I thought,
now there's one for each
of them or both
at once, out here in the wood,

taking it into my mouth.
Then them in the trailer scared,
listening for a second shot,
and me palate, brains, the whole

top of my head
blown clear at last,
clear right up
through the trees,

a roar I didn't even
hear. Though that
crazy I'm not. Not yet.
I'm just scary

enough to crouch waiting out
in the dark, wanting to
sneak up across
that brilliant yard ghostly

as Victor Charlie through
our frags. And kneel
resting my forehead on
the trailer's

cold aluminum skin,
feeling the movements
of them in there,
her with her glasses off,

eyes shut
tight and frowning that way,
she has like she was
trying to recall a face.

And him jerking
away above her with some
look of savage
concentration.

8.

(Linda Ellen Ball)

Power Lines

At the sink I can stare
from the kitchen window
at the girder
legs and struts of the power lines

straddled: okay, they're
outside our land. But so
damn close the nearest I can't see
the top unless I stoop.

I see the others whole,
though, getting littler,
astride across the whole
damn country, swathe-cut

through forest and
over pasture-land.
And I think again what
Sherrill said

when I told her how I hadn't
been too good lately,
migraines and not
sleeping and anxiety

and such. I thought
maybe it was the way things
been with me and Wes.
She said, *No. It ain't your*

tension. It's high voltage.
It's them power
lines. They'll mess up
your body's electric

fields just like a car radio.
Said she read about it. They ran
tests. And found how folk who
live under them cables

get a better chance at everything.
Leukemia. Mental problems.
Cancer. *That all?* I
said. But when I told Wes

he got mad and went
and switched the room-light
on in daytime. *See that?*
That's all

those cable lines is
carrying, he said. *Juice.*
In a rage, because I know
he hates them pylons too,

only he can't endure the irk
to think of what we paid
to buy this place and now
all that barbed wire

and angle iron outside
our windows and stretching
twenty miles off in plain view
to Harrisburg. *Don't*

blame every headache or
P.M.T. on the fucking power
company, that's all, he
said. *Electricity ain't*

Agent Orange. He laughed. *Look*
at me. I've had it all. For years.
Depressions. Dreads.
Insomnias. The places

I grew them, he said, *you*
wouldn't even see a lit
bulb at night, nor any
power to light one.

But I looked out at them power lines
next day and thought,
He's wrong. He just won't
admit as much. Or can't. Because

it would break his heart surely
to believe that all
of that and all of
this too was for

nothing, like everything
you ever tried or did after
that war was cursed. As if
what put them power lines

up outside our window and
what sent him off into
that jungle wasn't just
the same damn uniform thing.

9.

(Wesley Reece Ball)

Carrying A Torch

Like the sergeant said:
Never leave
a doorway that ain't burning...
We was all Local Boys —

but not from any ville round there.
My lighter was a Zippo made
in Bradford Pennsylvania,
came guaranteed against

repair for life.
It kept right through
my eleven months
the closing snap

a good knife,
and used up more
gas than a jeep.
It was like the claymore mine,

the needle bomb,
the fiery glory
of napalm:
we had the brains

and the machine
behind us.
Mine had my initials
drill-etched on it.

(I want to hear
it crackle,
the lieutenant said.
The whole damn place.)

Much later I thought
of the trapped
pigs squealing and the burning
rice that was all

those suckers had,
the oxen machinegunned
from the lifting chopper
for pure sport.

I left my Zippo on a bar-top
that first night in
The World and out
of uniform,

lonely drunk and
carrying a torch for
any girl
in Lewistown, Pee Ay.

10.
(Wesley Reece Ball)

Dreamback

In my dream she is
still running
in her black pyjamas.
If they don't stop

on a call, Lieutenant
Marino'd told us,
*you can make up your
mind or not to shoot.*

*Just take your time. Pick
one out and make
sure.* Right the way
across that waving

field I made up
mine. But when we
got to her it
was a girl. Sixteen? *This*

must be yours, Lynch
said. And licked
his finger, chalked
One on the air.

He toed her over, face
up. *Hell of a shot,
man.* (This from a boy
brought up on

rifles in the woods.)
And then
— that Tennessee
hick grin,

the missing tooth —,
Why don't you
fuck her?
She's still warm....

In my dream,
though, the bullets
veer away, I can
follow them by eye

as big as curve balls.
Or they lift and
hang above
her like a frisbee

on that wind across
the rice.
And when I turn
her over her face

is an old woman's,
the eyes open.
She puts her arms up
to me, draws

me down and says
I'm yours...
I don't need no Dr Freud or
fucking V.A. shrink to

work this out. But
what makes me cry
is: what is it
in us that longs so

to bring down
a running thing,
as if to
just see if we can?

Acknowledgements

Radio 3, *The Southern Review*, *New England Review & Breadloaf Quarterly*, *Poetry Review*, *Poetry Wales*, *The Archive*, *The Rialto*, *The North*, *Proposition*, *The Bright Field* (Carcanet), *The Malahat Review*, *Ambit*, *Proposition: Zeitschrift für Literatur*, *English Studies* (Centre Universitaire de Luxembourg), *The Urgency of Identity: Contemporary English-Language Poetry From Wales* (Northwestern University Press).